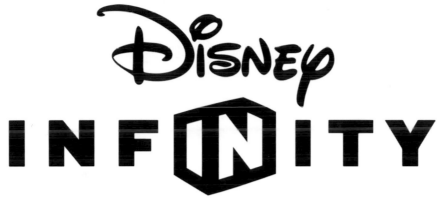

INFINITE POSSIBILITIES. ENDLESS FUN.

THE ESSENTIAL GUIDE

Written by **Catherine Saunders**

Contents

Introduction

Step into a world of action and adventure! Come and meet the bravest heroes, the meanest villains and the kookiest sidekicks.

Travel from the seven seas to the Wild West, from a world where scaring is big business to a distant planet inhabited by green aliens. Make friends with princesses, tow trucks, pirates and monsters – and remember to pack your coolest gadgets and your craziest vehicles.

Are you ready? Anything is possible here.

Jack Sparrow

Captain of a renowned pirate ship and scourge of the Royal Navy, Jack Sparrow is the most famous pirate in the seven seas. He has been on many adventures, from searching for cursed Aztec gold to fighting the fearsome beast, the Kraken. One thing's for sure, Captain Jack always has a daring plan.

All aboard!

Jack Sparrow's ship is 50 metres (165 feet) long and the second fastest in the Caribbean. Her hull is a bit scorched and her sails a little ragged, but this black ship is Jack Sparrow's pride and joy.

True or False?

Captain Jack Sparrow wants to control the seven seas.

False. Jack believes the seas should be free for whoever wishes to set sail on them. He is on a mission to make the seas free to all.

Swashbuckler

Captain Jack is a skilled swordsman, which is handy as he often finds himself in the middle of a sword fight! Thanks to a combination of quick wits and nimble footwork, even huge sea monsters like Maccus are no match for him.

Jack hates to be seen without his hat!

Long-bladed sword so Jack can reach further in battle

Pirate dream

Jack Sparrow is a simple pirate. All he wants is his beloved ship and the freedom to sail her anywhere he likes. Unfortunately, the seven seas are full of other pirates, the Royal Navy and terrifying monsters, such as the Kraken.

Compass doesn't point north, because it points to your heart's desire.

A new team

Jack Sparrow can be very charming when he needs to be. That's how he convinced Mike the Scarer and Mrs Incredible to join him on a treasure hunt. Mike has a weapon that even Jack hasn't tried yet – fireworks!

Well-worn pirate boots

Meet the Pirates

The Caribbean is home to a motley crew of pirates and their ships. Whether virtuous or wicked, most pirates spend their time on exciting adventures. Some are famed for their loyalty and bravery, while others count themselves lucky to still be alive.

Davy Jones

These days Davy Jones is more sea monster than human, and he roams the sea looking for sailors to join his cursed crew.

Hector Barbossa

Jack Sparrow's former first mate is a true pirate. He changes sides so often that no one can ever really trust him.

Tough job

A pirate's life is exciting, but dangerous. They're always being attacked by sea monsters or chased by the Navy. People never seem to give up their treasure without a fight!

Pintel

He might not be the smartest pirate in the ocean, but Pintel has managed to survive an Aztec curse and an encounter with the Kraken.

Faithful first mate

Jack Sparrow can usually depend on Joshamee Gibbs – he's as honest as any pirate can be. Gibbs did once leave Jack stranded on a desert island, but he was very sorry about it!

Joshamee Gibbs

First mate Gibbs has sailed the seven seas several times. He knows his way around a ship – and around the Caribbean!

Ragetti

This dopey, one-eyed pirate makes his pal Pintel look like a genius, but he's very good at following orders.

Rooftop Duel

With two crews trying to find the same treasure, they're bound to cross paths occasionally. Jack does everything he can to stop Davy Jones from piecing together the Kraken's Bane.

The old castle is said to conceal many treasures...

Jack must plan his escape well, as the exits are guarded.

Tia Dalma's house. Magic and mystery can be found here!

Bell tower. If the bell rings, Jack should flee while he can!

I am one of Captain Jack's oldest friends. I will help him find the Kraken's Bane!

Tia Dalma, Caribbean magician

Cursed Crew

Davy Jones can't sail his ship alone, he has a cursed crew to help him. Like their tentacled captain, Driftwood, Maccus, Clam and Turtle are less than human, and really mean. Keep clear!

A pirate ship waits at the docks in Dead Man's Cove.

Buccaneer Bay

This bay is a popular pirate hangout and it is rumoured that a missing piece of Kraken's Bane might be hidden here. Jack plans to sneak in and find it, but he must be careful – it looks like the bay is already under attack!

Caribbean Curse

Davy Jones has unleashed the terrifying Kraken, an enormous sea monster who can swallow ships whole. Captain Jack Sparrow and his pirate crew must find the only weapon that can defeat the fearsome beast, the Kraken's Bane. There's only one problem – they don't know where it is!

9

A Pirate's Life For Me

Ahoy there me hearties! Captain Jack Sparrow is wanting some new crew members and he's asked me, his old pal Joshamee Gibbs, to find 'em. We're looking for the scurviest seadogs, the dastardliest deck hands and the mouldiest mutineers. In other words, we be needing pirates. Arrrrr you up to the job?

Pillage and plunder

Do you have a nose for treasure and an eye for a quick escape? Nothing beats the thrill of finding a treasure map and setting off on an adventure. But if the Navy catch up with ye, you'd better have a clever plan or they'll throw you in gaol.

Mast

The masts hold the sails up and every pirate must be able to climb to the top.

Be ruthless

Do you have what it takes to be a pirate? There are no rules for pirates (the Pirates' Code is more like guidelines, you see), so you have to be clever, tough and willing to betray your pals for a bit of treasure – just like Davy Jones.

Sailing the seven seas

From the moment the first mate (that's me) wakes you up in the morning you'll be working hard. The decks need scrubbing, the sails need hoisting and the rigging needs climbing. Life on the ocean is rough. And as for the food, well, I just hopes you like weevils...

Crow's nest

If you've got a head for heights, I'll send you up here to keep a lookout for land, or the Navy.

Pirate lingo

Can you speak like a pirate? Captain Jack and I didn't get where we are today by sounding like lily-livered land lubbers. Here are a few pirate words to help ye out.

Ahoy! – hello
Arrrrr – all-purpose pirate word
Aye – yes
Me – my
Me hearties – my friends
Ye – you

Lateen sail

This triangular sail catches the wind in the fore and aft – that means both sides, in case ye didn't know.

Anchor

When I yell "Drop anchor!" ye must wind this metal hook until it hits the sea bed.

Cannons

Ready, aim, fire! You'll need strong arms to load, fire and reload the one-ton cannons that point out of these portholes.

WHAT HAPPENS WHEN...

...a pirate meets a princess, a superhero hits the race track or a monster takes a trip to space? Anything is possible, but one thing's for sure – it is going to be a thrilling adventure.

Tea party

Is this the craziest tea party ever? Jessie, Wreck-it Ralph, Sulley, Mr Incredible and a cute little alien decide to take time out from their hectic schedules to catch up over some tea and cakes.

Monstrous moves

When Captain Jack Sparrow borrows Cinderella's carriage, he customises it with some monster truck tyres so he can outrun Barbossa. It's so speedy he even zooms past Sulley and Lightning McQueen.

Air race

Syndrome hates losing, but Elsa and the Incredicopter look to have beaten him into second place. Who knew that Elsa was such a flying ace?

Trusty steeds

The Lone Ranger and Tonto are searching for their missing horses. Mrs Incredible and Mike turn up to help – and they've brought along some very interesting rides, too!

Incredible pit crew

Lightning knows that a great pit crew can be the difference between winning and losing. With the Incredibles on his team, his rivals don't stand a chance!

The Incredibles

There's one word to describe this family – Incredible! They're an awesome super-powered, supervillain-fighting team. However, when they're not wearing their super suits, they are just like any other family.

Mrs Incredible

Flying a plane, defeating bad guys and whipping up a delicious dinner are all in a day's work for Super Mum, Mrs Incredible.

Flexible mum

Mrs Incredible has a surprising body. She can bend it to any shape or stretch it up to 91 metres (300 feet) but it always snaps back to its original size.

Violet

Violet is super shy, but being a hero gives her confidence. Maybe her powers are pretty cool, after all.

Fun Fact

Each of the Incredibles has a unique power: Mr Incredible is super strong, Mrs Incredible is super stretchy, Violet can become invisible and create force fields and Dash is super fast.

14

Mr Incredible

Mr Incredible is the strongest Super in the world. He can lift huge weights and his body is almost invulnerable.

Super dad

Mr Incredible has no problem beating up omnidroids, but when it comes to being a parent, he finds that super tough. Battling bad guys is much easier than making his kids do their homework!

Dash

He's the fastest 10-year-old on Larth, and he knows it. Dash loves to show off – he can even run on water!

Syndrome

This evil genius has a huge grudge against Mr Incredible, and it's about to be payback time. Syndrome has spent years creating an arsenal of evil inventions, and he plans to show his Super enemy just how smart and powerful he is.

"I'm your nemesis!"

An enormously evil hairstyle

A beautiful mind

Syndrome recruited brainy Mirage to help him get information on Mr Incredible and other Supers. However, when she realised her boss's evil plan, Mirage switched sides.

Inner-heeled boots add a few extra inches

Cape – for a very villainous look

Fan or enemy?

Syndrome's real name is Buddy Pine and as a kid he was Mr Incredible's biggest fan. In fact, he dreamed of being the Super's sidekick, Incrediboy. When Mr Incredible rejected him, Buddy became very bitter. And very evil.

Omnidroids

Syndrome's secret weapon is an intelligent robot that can analyse any Super's powers and then recreate them. It will make Syndrome invincible!

Buddy Pine's Revenge Checklist

- ☑ Choose supervillain name and design awesome costume.
- ☑ Invent evil robots and weapons.
- ☐ Destroy Mr Incredible.

Finding new targets

Syndrome loves testing out new toys. Fortunately, the Lone Ranger, Tonto and Woody can outrun the pink glow urchins before they make their horses swell up!

17

Super statue

At the front of the NSA building, there is a large statue commemorating the heroic work of the Agency's greatest ever Super – the famous hero, Mr Incredible.

Docks drama

The city's docks are a prime location for criminal activity. Once, a group of supervillain prisoners were being loaded onto a ship – but Syndrome freed them. Mr Incredible raced to the crime scene.

Metroville's tallest building – Metroville Bank – is a top target.

An attack on the city's water tanks would be terrible!

The streets are pretty empty since Syndrome arrived.

Concerned citizens

The citizens of Metroville want a peaceful life. They trust the NSA and the Incredibles to keep their city safe.

Metroville

Welcome to Metroville, a friendly, modern city by the ocean. It's a great place to be, and a safe one too, thanks to the Incredibles, who live here. These super-powered heroes work for the National Supers Agency (NSA), which has its high-tech headquarters in Metroville.

Advertisement board promises a villain-free holiday.

Supers fight back

The Incredibles know every inch of Metroville. When Syndrome's omnidroid army attacks, the Supers defend the streets. A few buildings might be destroyed during battle, but at least the citizens are safe!

It's up to the NSA and the Supers to keep Metroville safe. Syndrome beware!

Rick Dicker, NSA agent

19

Incredible Vehicles

The Incredibles have a range of awesome super powers, but even they need a little help getting around sometimes. The geniuses at the NSA have built a fleet of incredible vehicles for them. With these amazing contraptions, villains like Syndrome don't stand a chance.

Violet glides silently toward an omnidroid.

Glide pack

For speedy, smooth flying over short distances, this glide pack is just the thing every Super needs. Best of all it is completely silent, so supervillains never hear it coming!

Lightweight wings

Simple backpack design

Minimal air resistance

Incredicar

Mr Incredible loves this car – it's sleek and fast, and it looks cool. At the push of a button it can locate a target, work out a route and even drive itself there in "autodrive" mode.

Aerodynamic curves

The Incredicar is fireproof, bulletproof, rocket proof and bomb proof.

Reinforced bumper

Low-volume rotors

Dash might be the fastest thing on land, but he can't fly. Luckily, the Incredicopter can help him defeat the omnidroids.

Incredicopter

This single-person craft needs a pilot with fast reflexes – so it is a perfect vehicle for any Super. Violet loves flying the Incredicopter, when Dash gives her a turn.

All-terrain landing pads

Hover board

In his younger days, Mr Incredible was a keen surfer and talented skateboarder. Nowadays he doesn't need waves or wheels, thanks to this rocket-powered hover board.

Magnetic platform

The hover board can travel over land or sea.

Air jets under base

Perfectly balanced

Pick Your Perfect Partner

Adventures are much more fun if you have a best buddy to share them with. A good pal will also help you if you are in danger, and when it comes to getting out of a difficult situation, two heads are always better then one. Answer these questions to find your perfect match. The results may surprise you...

START

Are you looking for a big adventure?

Are you quiet or talkative?

QUIET

NO

NO

Are you a natural leader?

YES

NO

Can you do many things at once?

YES

Tonto

YES →

You're a quiet, thoughtful person who really cares about wildlife and the great outdoors. You're a loyal friend who always tries to do the right thing. Your perfect partner is Tonto.

Do you like nature?

Mater

NO →

You have a very kind heart but you like playing tricks. You love visiting new places and are extremely chatty. Have some good, old-fashioned fun with Mater.

TALKATIVE

YES →

Rapunzel

You are a friendly person who lives life to the full. You are reliable and trustworthy – and will do anything for your friends. Pair up with Rapunzel for many fun-filled adventures.

Do you like playing pranks?

NO →

Buzz Lightyear

YES

You like adventure and were born to lead. You have lots of friends, but can sometimes be a bit too serious. Lighten up and let loose with Buzz Lightyear!

NO

Mrs Incredible

Are you easygoing?

YES →

You are busy and hard-working, and you know how to juggle many tasks at once. You're strong and independent, but you are also easygoing. You should hang out with Mrs Incredible!

Sulley sometimes thinks his blue eyes aren't particularly scary.

Mike and Sulley

These two Scarers are best friends, but they didn't always see eye to eye. When they studied Scaring at Monsters University, Mike and Sulley were rivals. It was only when they were both expelled from MU that they learned how to work together. Nowadays they are an unbeatable scare team.

Student prank

During Fear-it Week at MU, Mike had lots of fun with his toilet paper launcher. He toilet-papered half of his class before anyone caught up with him.

Scare practice

A Scarer's greatest weapon is a loud roar. Sulley got plenty of practice at MU, but his fellow students weren't too happy about it!

24

Huge, hairy legs

New monster in town!

Mike and Sulley are scary, but they can't compete with a real-life sea monster! Davy Jones wants to teach them a thing or two, but Mike and Sulley can't get away fast enough!

"YOU DON'T NEED TO STUDY SCARING, YOU JUST DO IT!"

Only one eye, but big enough to see for miles!

FUN FACT

Mike and Sulley are so good at scaring, their friends have invited them camping – so they can tell some super scary stories round the camp fire! Rapunzel can't wait, although she is a bit scared...

Being monstrous

Sulley is huge and hairy and he comes from a family of Scarers, so scaring came naturally to him. Mike had to work much harder to become a terrifying Scarer – it's not easy to scare people when you're small and cute.

Mike used to get teased about his skinny, green legs.

25

Scare Students

Monsters University is a place where monsters can be moulded into even bigger monsters, but only if they can handle the creepy curriculum. Not everyone is cut out to be a Scarer, but those that fail the Scare Programme are always welcome in the Oozma Kappa fraternity.

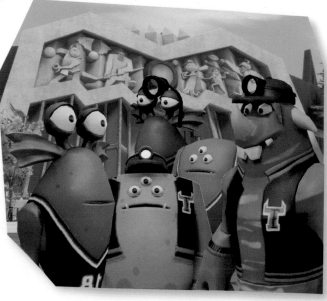

Rotten rivals

The students of Fear Tech are determined to beat MU in this year's Fear-it Week, and they'll try any mean trick to do it. These guys are sneaky, as well as scary.

Freaky freshman

This fang-toothed, winged monster looks fierce, but he's more scared than Scarer.

Art

Philosophy major and yoga fan Art is a monster with a mysterious past and a crazy personality. He's more into reflexology than roaring.

Scare off

MU's big rivals are Fear Tech. The two schools battle it out during Fear-it Week. Competition is fierce, and so are the late-night pranks, which include Sulley toilet-papering Fear Tech's statue.

Terri and Terry

The only thing these inseparable brothers agree on is their dream of becoming Scarers. The rest of the time, they just argue.

The Oozma Kappa fraternity will let anybody in.

False. Most monsters are welcome in Oozma Kappa – but they must show a dedication to scaring.

TRUE OR FALSE?

Randy

Reserved Randy doesn't even know how scary he looks, until he is invited to join MU's coolest fraternity – Roar Omega Roar.

Squishy

Squishy is Oozma Kappa's proudest member. What he lacks in scare abilities, he makes up for in cheerfulness!

Quad biking

The quad in the centre of the MU campus is a popular place for students to hang out after class. Sulley thinks he is a natural Scarer so he often cuts class and roars around the quad on Mike's bike.

Shhh!

There's more to being a Scarer than looking fierce – it takes brains, too. The MU library is full of Scaring books. Watch out though, it's also the perfect place for a Fear Tech prank...

Campus Tour

Monsters University in Monstropolis is the number one school for students who are serious about Scaring. Run by the terrifying Dean Hardscrabble, MU also offers courses in science, engineering and business for those who aren't quite scary enough.

School clock – it's always time to scare!

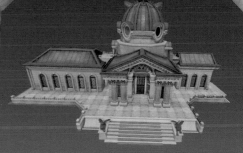

School of Scaring
This is the most famous building on campus – the School of Scaring. Here generations of monsters have learned how to roar, make scary faces and creep up on people. BOO!

Monstrous fountain – a prime pranking spot.

Banners advertise an array of monstrous events to look forward to.

SCHOOL OF SCARING

Everyone's welcome at MU. I used to be a salesman – and now I'm studying Scaring!

Don Carlton, president of Oozma Kappa fraternity

Randy's Pranks

For monsters like Randy, college is not easy. Scaring doesn't come naturally to him, so Randy puts in lots of extra time working on pranks to practise his Scaring skills. Pranks are fun – as long as they're aimed at someone else! Here are some of Randy's best.

PAINTBALL GUN

This is a classic prank. Find a nice high spot, such as the clocktower, where no one can see you. Then "splat!" hit unsuspecting monsters with a blob of paint.

They won't suspect a thing! Ha ha!

Small enough to hide behind your back!

GIVE 'EM A HAND LAUNCHER

This one works a treat, every time. Someone walks past this ordinary-looking billboard and "wham!" It socks them right in the kisser.

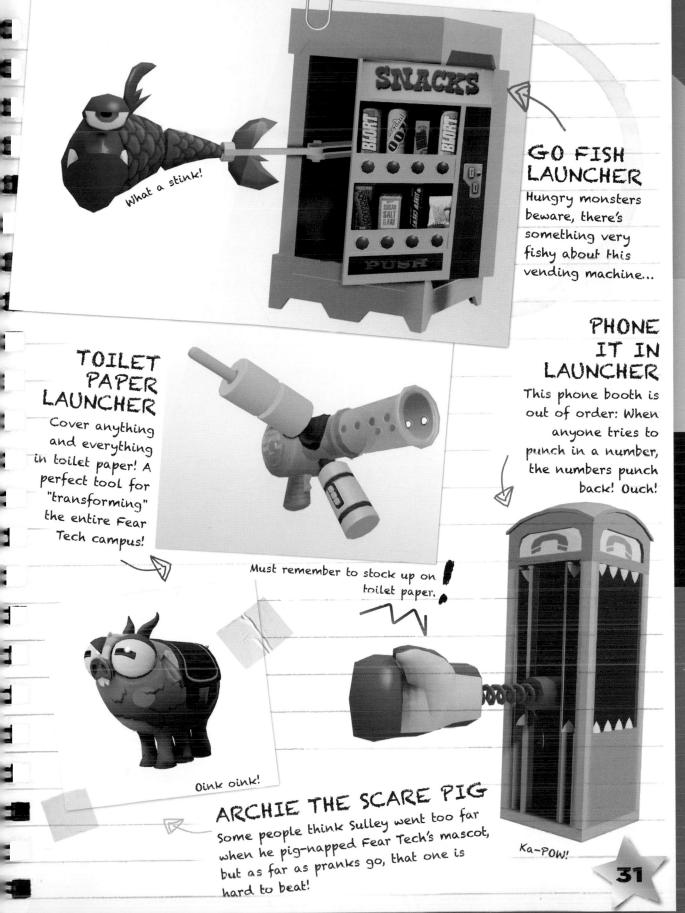

What a stink!

GO FISH LAUNCHER

Hungry monsters beware, there's something very fishy about this vending machine...

PHONE IT IN LAUNCHER

This phone booth is out of order: When anyone tries to punch in a number, the numbers punch back! Ouch!

TOILET PAPER LAUNCHER

Cover anything and everything in toilet paper! A perfect tool for "transforming" the entire Fear Tech campus!

Must remember to stock up on toilet paper.

Oink oink!

ARCHIE THE SCARE PIG

Some people think Sulley went too far when he pig-napped Fear Tech's mascot, but as far as pranks go, that one is hard to beat!

Ka-POW!

31

SULLEY'S New Friends

Sulley has many monster friends from his university days, but there is nothing better than making new pals. Sulley is always ready to grab his new buddies and jump into an adventure – and Sulley's friends know that together, they will have a great time!

Rapunzel

Rapunzel has spent most of her life in a tower, and now that she's finally busted out, it's even better than she dreamed it would be. When she first met Sulley, they joined forces with Jessie and Mr Incredible for a crazy paintball fight!

Mickey Mouse

When Mickey found out that Sulley and Mater love driving as much as he does, he was thrilled! On the track, they are fierce rivals, but off the track they are great friends.

Captain Jack Sparrow

Jack Sparrow loves the feeling of wind in his long hair! He formed a flying club together with his friends Sulley and Mr Incredible.

Mr Incredible

Sometimes only a fellow tough guy can relate to the pressures of being a hero. Sulley and the Lone Ranger understand how Mr Incredible feels. They all enjoy de-stressing on an assault course.

Jessie

Jessie was once searching for a stolen magic lamp when Sulley said he would help her out. Of course, they found it in the end.

Lightning McQueen

He might have won four Piston Cups and a World Grand Prix, but racing legend Lightning McQueen knows that his greatest prize was ending up in Radiator Springs. Lightning has driven all around the globe, but he's happiest at home, surrounded by all his pals.

Did You Know?

During his career, Lightning has learned that friendship is more important than winning. That is why he doesn't mind when one of his new friends, super speedy Dash Incredible, beats him in a race!

New star

An International Race Invitational is coming to Radiator Springs, and Luigi, a little yellow Fiat, has been selected to race. Race pro Lightning helps his pal get ready.

Hot wheels

Lightning once joined Mr Incredible, Jack Skellington, Syndrome and Buzz Lightyear for a game of fire football. He loved it! And not just because his team won 10–0.

Lightyear all-weather race tyres

Race ready

Although he's not about to enter a race, Lightning still likes to keep race-fit. He does 100 laps every morning and makes sure his engine is in peak condition. A champion is always ready to race!

Back seat driver

Lightning isn't the centre of attention right now, and that's fine with him. With so much free time, Lightning will get the chance to relax with his friends – and he can't wait to be a racing fan for once!

"Ready to see where the road takes me."

Determined expression

Lightning is famous for his red and yellow paint job.

35

Fleet of Cars

Radiator Springs is the hottest place to be right now. It's about to host the International Race Invitational, so some of the greatest cars in the world are roaring into town. The friendly residents can't wait to make them feel right at home.

Business opportunity

Tow Mater owns the only salvage yard in Radiator Springs. He might be rusty, but he's no fool – this race could mean big business for him. He might finally be able to afford a new paint job!

Tyre fan

Luigi is the owner of Casa Della Tires, but he's about to take centre stage as Radiator Springs' competitor in the International Race Invitational.

Talkative truck

Mater has travelled the world with his best pal Lightning McQueen. He can't wait to tell the visitors all his amazing stories!

Checking the course

Holley can't shake the feeling that something bad is about to happen, so she checks the race circuit with Mater and Lightning.

True or False?

Radiator Springs is a very friendly place.

True. Even though some of the visiting cars are not exactly friendly, the locals want them to enjoy their stay!

Dirty car

Chick Hicks tricked his way to a Piston Cup trophy and he's determined to win the International Race Invitational. It's a shame he wasn't even invited.

Spy car

Rookie spy Holley is looking forward to a holiday in Radiator Springs, but a good spy is always prepared for action!

European champion

Francesco Bernoulli has no doubt about who's going to win the race – him! He is super confident, and super arrogant.

Casa Della Tires

Whether you've got a tyre emergency or you just need a new look, Casa Della Tires is the place to go. Owners Luigi and Guido know everything there is to know about tyres.

Enjoy great views of the Cadillac mountain range.

Welcome to Radiator Springs – home to the world's most delicious organic fuel!

Fillmore, Radiator Springs resident

Cozy Cone Motel

Radiator Springs' best (and only) motel offers comfortable, yet affordable rooms, with plenty of off-street parking. Book early to avoid disappointment.

Courthouse

The citizens of Radiator Springs are extremely law-abiding so they don't use the courthouse very often. In fact, no one has been inside it since Lightning McQueen first crashed into town.

Flo's V8 Café – the place to relax and sip refreshing oil drinks.

House of Body Art – run by airbrush expert Ramone.

A Tourist's Guide to Radiator Springs

When Lightning McQueen first came to Radiator Springs, it was a quiet, sleepy town on the edge of the desert. Now, thanks to the International Race Invitational, it is a tourist hotspot. Come and explore the sights of Radiator Springs!

39

Top Racing Tips

Recently, several great and not-so-great race cars have stopped at Flo's V8 Café for an oil shake or a gas smoothie. Before they know it, they are spilling all their problems – and their racing secrets. Flo has collected lots of useful racing knowledge...

Good listener

When cars talk to Flo, she always listens. In Radiator Springs, a lot of conversations revolve around racing, so you could say that Flo has become a bit of an expert!

FLO'S TOP TIPS

Holley keeps some blasters handy for emergencies.

✳ "It's all about the element of surprise."
– Holley

Driving backwards is lots of fun! (Even if it's not so fast!)

✳ "I don't know why more cars don't drive backwards. It's fun!"
– Mater

✳ "The secret to win every race is to have the best tyres."
– Luigi

✳ "A cool paint job will help you feel like a winner – even before the race."
– Ramone

✳ "A race car has got to look good on the track. Can't disappoint the fans."
– Lightning (before he came to Radiator Springs)

Lightning always drives better when Holley and Mater are around.

✳ "Being part of a great team is what counts."
– Lightning (now)

✳ "Winning is everything! How does not matter."
– Francesco

Francesco doesn't care about making friends.

✳ "Always make sure you have enough fuel – from Flo's V8 Café, naturally."
– Flo

41

Sulley

Sorcerer's
Apprentice Mickey

Jack
Skellington

Elsa

Stay cool
Elsa can create and control ice.
In a race against some of her
fastest friends, she must keep
her cool – if she doesn't, her
rivals might get frozen out!

Syndrome

Keep it real
Syndrome has spent his life
inventing evil gadgets and
vehicles. However, sometimes
the simple, old-fashioned ways
are best, such as riding
Maximus, the horse.

Don't look down!

Sulley is no mini-monster, so he needs a flying machine that can carry his furry bulk. Dumbo, a mechanical flying elephant, fits the bill perfectly. It looks super cute, too!

Mix and match

Mickey likes to "borrow" things. First it was a magical sorcerer's hat, then it was Mr Incredible's car. Mickey actually has a red jalopy of his own, but the Incredicar is much faster!

Break the mould

Sometimes Jack Skellington needs a break from scaring people. So, he borrows Mr Incredible's hover board and heads off on a crazy new adventure.

Crazy Races

Sometimes to get ahead, you need to think outside the box. Try something new, embrace the unexpected or hop on board the unusual. Sulley, Mickey, Jack Skellington, Elsa and Syndrome have all done just that, and they can't wait to race. Ready, steady, go!

Lone Ranger and Tonto

Lawyer John Reid could not stand by and let criminals attack his town, so he became masked crime-fighter, the Lone Ranger. Comanche warrior Tonto wants peace, but he may have to fight to achieve it. Together, this daring duo are determined to make the Wild West a safer place. Outlaws beware!

Faithful stallions

Tonto and the Lone Ranger don't work alone. Scout, Tonto's horse, always shows Tonto the right path, while Silver, the fastest horse in the West, never lets the Lone Ranger down.

Mask

Being the Lone Ranger is a dangerous job so John Reid keeps his true identity a secret behind his black mask. Only Tonto knows the truth.

Dark clothes so the Lone Ranger can keep a low profile

44

Showdown

The Lone Ranger is determined to protect his home town, Colby, from outlaws. He is an ace marksman and can hit even the smallest target from the other side of town. The bad guys don't stand a chance.

Cowgirl to the rescue

When Jessie heard that her pals in the Wild West were having trouble, the sassy cowgirl didn't hesitate. She'll darn-tootin' show those outlaws a thing or two!

Tonto wears a black crow on his headdress.

"How can we help, Sheriff?"

Brave team

John Reid believes in law and order and Tonto is a spiritual man who loves animals and nature. They are men of honour and justice, but sometimes, in the Wild West, justice is a battle.

Soft shoes for sneaking up on villains

45

Cavendish Gang

Butch Cavendish is one mean outlaw. He wants power and riches – so he is planning to take control of the trains and gold mines of the Wild West. Butch has a crew of gun-toting, law-breaking thugs to help him. The greedy gang will stop at nothing to get what they want.

Bandit leader

Butch Cavendish has big plans. He wants to be rich, powerful and the most wanted man in the Wild West.

Under attack

The townsfolk of Colby are no match for the Cavendish Gang, but the Sheriff won't give up his town without a fight. He calls in Colby's very own crime-fighting hero – the Lone Ranger.

Formidable firepower

The Cavendish Gang rarely loses a gun battle, thanks to this ten-barrel gatling gun. Dynamite is another favourite weapon – this stash is going to blow up the railroad!

Loyal thug

Square-jawed and moody-looking, this outlaw never smiles. Being bad is a very serious business!

Brawn not brains

This cowboy might not be very smart, but he is very strong and does whatever Butch orders him to.

Explosives expert

This bearded bandit always carries a stick or two of dynamite wherever he goes. He loves blowing things up.

Colby Rooming House – the only restaurant, bar and hotel in town.

The good guys

The Lone Ranger and Tonto ride into town, ready to defend Colby from the Cavendish Gang. The townspeople are scared, but they help the Lone Ranger any way they can.

Local furniture store doubles as the undertaker.

RESTAURANT

COLBY ROOMING HOUSE

The only way out

If Butch and his men succeed in taking over the railroad, the only way out of Colby will be the stagecoach, which only stops in town once a week.

Wild West Showdown

The small frontier town of Colby is usually a quiet place where the townsfolk work hard, respect each other and obey the law. However, Butch Cavendish thinks it will make the perfect base for his band of outlaws, so he is going to take control of the town – by force.

Prime location

Cavendish chose Colby because it's close to the railroad. After he's taken over the town, the railroad will be next. Butch knows that whoever controls the railroad, controls the Wild West.

Town laundry – the townsfolk bring their dirty clothes here.

Silver and Scout can always get a good feed at this stable.

There's no way I'm going to let Butch Cavendish just walk in and take over my town!

Red Harrington, local businesswoman and saloon owner

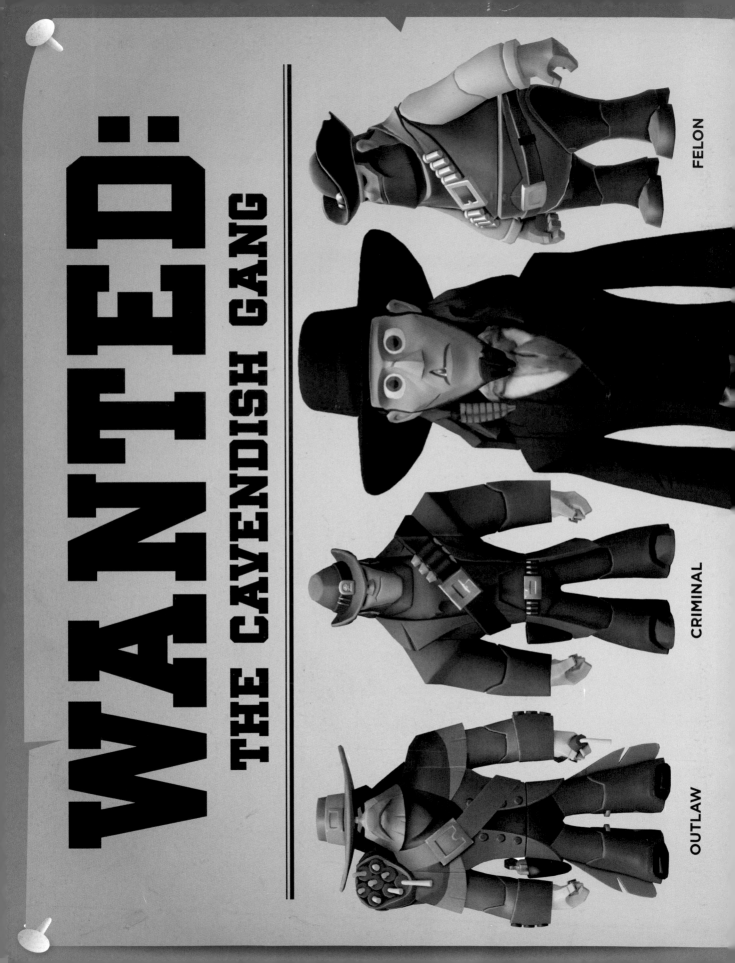

INFAMOUS BANDITS
(ARMED AND DANGEROUS)

Led by Butch Cavendish, these wicked outlaws are accused of terrorising the town of Colby, attacking the railroad and causing chaos in the Wild West. They must be brought to justice.

These men are armed and extremely dangerous. If you see them, please report it to your Sheriff. Do not confront them.

BUTCH CAVENDISH

Do not engage the Cavendish Gang in combat as they are known to carry explosives and a gatling gun.

It is strongly advised that people do not travel alone. It is not safe.

Train passengers beware

The Cavendish Gang have already attacked the railroad and they will do so again. Passengers should only undertake essential journeys.

Be Prepared

So, you're off on an adventure, but you don't know where it might take you or who you might meet. Question: What should you take with you? Answer: Everything you can carry! You just never know what you might need...

WALL•E's fire extinguisher

Strap on this fire extinguisher to boost your jumps with a little extra power. It's handy for a quick getaway, too.

Condor wings

Who says you can't fly? With these condor wings, you can glide about like a huge bird of prey.

Star Command blaster

It's always best to be prepared to fight. This weapon can destroy an omnidroid with just three shots, but it needs to be reloaded after every six shots.

Slingshot

You might need to practise with this gadget. If you get it right, you can use it to launch small objects over great distances.

Sticky hand

You can be as bendy as Mrs Incredible with this sticky gadget. It's great for climbing or jumping – just shoot, watch it stick and then swing.

Cruella de Vil's car

This is a great way to travel and it has plenty of trunk space to store all your other gadgets. You just have to get permission to borrow it from that crazy dog-hater Cruella de Vil.

Invisinator

Dr Doofenshmirtz's useful invention will make you temporarily invisible, but you might not remember exactly where you packed it!

Carl Fredricksen's cane

This homemade cane with tennis balls makes a useful weapon, and it might also come in handy if you ever need a walking aid.

Zero Point Energy gauntlet

This weapon is awesome! Use its energy field to pick up enemies or objects and then throw them out of your way.

Mania gun

Blast bad guys with this powerful mania gun. It will send them crazy and give you time to escape.

Flamingo croquet mallet

This bird-shaped mallet is perfect if you happen to find yourself in the middle of a game of croquet. It also makes a useful weapon. Thunk!

Box of fireworks

Create a diversion with these rockets and firecrackers, or just have an awesome party!

Party cannon

This cannon can shoot fireworks or confetti, or even both at the same time. It is perfect if you want to make a stylish entrance.

Goo shrinker

Sometimes size matters, and if you need to gain a height or weight advantage just use the goo shrinker to cover your foes in goo – then they'll shrink to a more manageable size.

Woody

Sheriff Woody has learned that it's important to be versatile. He never knows where his next adventure might take him, from terrifying toy stores to sinister daycare centres. But there's one place that Woody hasn't visited yet – space. Fortunately his best friend Buzz Lightyear knows all about space...

Treasure trove

Others might be tempted to steal this valuable alien gold, but not Woody. The only treasure Woody cares about is his friends. He does everything he can to keep them safe, and together.

Space cowboy

When Woody and his friends receive a distress call from outer space, they leap into action. Woody never imagined they'd find an alien city!

True or False?

Woody knows all about space.

False. Woody has never been to space, but his best friend Buzz Lightyear is a space ranger.

Andy's name is written on Woody's boots

Top toy

Woody is a natural leader, which is why he was Andy's favourite toy. All the other toys look up to him. Woody doesn't always get it right first time, but he makes the smart decision in the end.

Gold sheriff's badge

The claw

Woody is always there when his best pal Buzz Lightyear needs him. This time, though, Woody has to rescue Mike Wazowski and several green aliens as well!

Cowboy boots with spurs

He might be a space ranger now, but Woody always dresses like a cowboy!

"Yee-haw! Giddyup, pardner!"

Woody's Gang

Meet Sheriff Woody's best friends. This gang of toys has been through many adventures together, from moving house to nearly being thrown out with the trash. They always look out for each other, but how will they handle a trip to space?

Buzz Lightyear

Brave space ranger Buzz likes to play by the rules. He is a natural leader, but sometimes needs his friends to remind him how to have fun.

Rex

He worries about his short arms, quiet roar and clumsy tail, but this timid tyrannosaurus rex is tougher than he thinks.

Hamm

This brainy porker is the smartest toy around. He just wishes that all the toys' adventures weren't quite so dangerous!

Top toys

Hamm and Rex approach problems very differently: Hamm likes to think things through, while Rex likes to jump right in. But that doesn't mean they aren't the best of friends!

A friend in me

Buzz and Jessie are great at dodging volcanic alien goo and saving planets. They have become close friends and are always looking out for each other.

Jessie

Yee-haw! This fun-loving cowgirl can never resist an adventure. She is brave and bold and will never let her fellow toys down.

Bullseye

Trusty toy horse Bullseye can gallop as fast as the wind. His hooves are also useful for working the TV remote.

Slinky Dog

Faithful, friendly and incredibly stretchy, Slinky Dog is a chilled-out canine. He is incredibly loyal to his good pal Sheriff Woody.

Oooooooh! We are in danger! Please save us Sheriff Woody and spaceman Buzz.

Green alien, inhabitant of a distant planet

Distress signal sent from satellite communication dish.

Little green people

This beautiful planet is home to millions of green aliens. The suns are always shining and there is hardly a dust cloud in the sky. Life was good until all the trouble with Zurg began.

New decoration centre – very popular with the aliens.

58

Alien Planet

Far out in the depths of space, this planet is under attack by the evil Emperor Zurg! The little green aliens who live here have one last hope: some of their citizens visited Earth a while back and met some brave toys. Will Woody, Buzz and the gang answer their distress call?

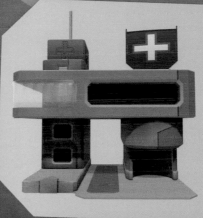

Home planet

The alien planet is quite similar to Earth. It has hospitals, schools and stores. Unlike Earth however, it also has a defence shield tower and an enormous goo-blasting volcano.

Research station analyses data from the nearby volcano.

Lovely lava

This planet is very safe, as long as you don't fall into any of the oozing volcanic goo. It is so sticky that you might not be able to escape. It is pretty smelly, too.

MISSION:
Protect the Planet

During his years with Star Command, space ranger Buzz Lightyear went on many exciting and dangerous missions. Now, he is preparing for his most daring space adventure yet, with his pals Woody, Jessie and the gang. Before they set off, Buzz has some expert advice to share.

1 ☑

CHECK THE AREA

It is important to conduct a full survey of the mission area, identifying the key locations and finding the safest spots. A good spaceman is always prepared.

2 ☑

PROTECT THE CITIZENS

The most important part of any mission is making sure that the citizens are safe. Buzz can communicate in many languages and he always likes to put the local population at ease.

☑ 3
DEFENCE IS BETTER THAN ATTACK

Battle should always be the last resort for a clever space ranger. Activate defence shields and negotiate with the enemy before resorting to a battle.

4 ☐
ALWAYS HAVE BACK UP

A good spaceman never works alone – everyone needs a trusty partner. During missions, Buzz looks out for his friends, and he will always be there to help them out.

5 ☐
KNOW YOUR ENEMY

Buzz has defeated the evil Emperor Zurg many times in the past and knows all the villain's weak spots. Unfortunately, Zurg is also Buzz's Dad, so things can get a little complicated...

Ralph's Day of Adventure

All his life, Wreck-it Ralph has been the bad guy of arcade games, but he's tired of it. He's off on an adventure today to show the world that he is really a good guy. Join him and find out who helps make this Ralph's best day ever!

Ralph is made for smashing and wrecking things. But he wants to show people that there is so much more to him.

10:02 AM

Wrecking truck

Ralph's big wrecking truck is the ideal size for him. It is perfect for crushing things, but this morning, Ralph decides to use it as a race car. Will he win the race against Syndrome?

12:18 PM

Being brave

Sulley doesn't meet many guys who are bigger than him, let alone braver. So he is keen to challenge Ralph to a fiery obstacle course. Ralph shows Sulley just how brave he is!

Joining in

Thanks to Ralph's mechanical building skills, Vanellope is finally able to do what she always wanted to – race. Her Candy Kart is much faster than Ralph's wrecking truck, but that's OK – nice guys don't have to finish first!

On the open road

Ralph loves going for a run. In the afternoon he meets a group of friendly aliens, who cheer him on. Ralph better watch where he's putting his feet though!

Brain box

The new Ralph has even decided to get in touch with his clever side. A game of life-sized chess really gets his brain juices flowing.

Reach for the sky

As evening falls, Ralph takes to the skies. His new pal Woody has been giving him flying lessons, and there is nothing Ralph loves more than exploring the world from above.

Ladies' man

Ralph didn't know that he had a romantic side. He hopes that Princess Anna will be impressed with his climbing and smashing skills. Unfortunately for Ralph, she's not.

Acknowledgements

LONDON, NEW YORK, MELBOURNE,
MUNICH and DELHI

Editor Shari Last
Senior Designer Lynne Moulding
Designers Alison Gardner, Lisa Robb, Toby Truphet
Design Assistant Elena Jarmoskaite
Managing Editor Laura Gilbert
Design Manager Maxine Pedliham
Publishing Manager Julie Ferris
Art Director Lisa Lanzarini
Publishing Director Simon Beecroft
Senior Pre-Production Producer Jennifer Murray
Producers Louise Daly, Danielle Smith

First published in Great Britain in 2014
by Dorling Kindersley Limited
80 Strand, London WC2R 0RL

10 9 8 7 6 5 4 3 2 1
001—196539—Mar/14

Page design copyright © 2014 Dorling Kindersley Limited
A Penguin Random House Company

A catalogue record for this book is available from the British Library.

ISBN: 978-1-40934-225-0

Colour reproduction by Alta Image, UK
Printed and bound in Slovakia by TBB, a.s.

Discover more at
www.dk.com
www.disney.com